Sacred Poems.

BY

N. P. WILLIS.

NEW YORK:
CLARK, AUSTIN & SMITH,
3 PARK ROW AND 3 ANN-STREET.
1853.

Preface.

After repeated publication in many different shapes, the following poems are now presented in a more convenient and cheaper form than ever before; and, in the call for this popular edition, the author cannot but find a gratifying approbation of the character and spirit of his writings. Most of them were first published with no expectation of the ordeal of such constant reproduction to public notice, and the author is well aware that their popularity arises in a great measure from the religious and moral tone of most of them, and from their having thus appealed to a prevalent taste which is in many ways the strength and beauty of his country. It is a happy and safe land where such qualities make a book more saleable. The poems within are commended, once more, gratefully and feelingly, to the American public.

N. P. WILLIS.

October, 1846.

Contents.

POEMS.

The Healing of the Daughter of Jairus.

Freshly the cool breath of the coming eve
Stole through the lattice, and the dying girl
Felt it upon her forehead. She had lain
Since the hot noontide in a breathless trance—
Her thin pale fingers clasp'd within the hand
Of the heart-broken Ruler, and her breast,
Like the dead marble, white and motionless.
The shadow of a leaf lay on her lips,
And, as it stirr'd with the awakening wind,
The dark lids lifted from her languid eyes,
And her slight fingers moved, and heavily
She turn'd upon her pillow. He was there—
The same loved, tireless watcher, and she look'd
Into his face until her sight grew dim
With the fast-falling tears ; and, with a sigh
Of tremulous weakness murmuring his name,

She gently drew his hand upon her lips,
And kiss'd it as she wept. The old man sunk
Upon his knees, and in the drapery
Of the rich curtains buried up his face;
And when the twilight fell, the silken folds
Stirr'd with his prayer, but the slight hand he held
Had ceased its pressure—and he could not hear,
In the dead, utter silence, that a breath
Came through her nostrils—and her temples gave
To his nice touch no pulse—and, at her mouth,
He held the lightest curl that on her neck
Lay with a mocking beauty, and his gaze
Ached with its deathly stillness. * * * * *

* * * * * * It was night—
And, softly, o'er the Sea of Galilee,
Danced the breeze-ridden ripples to the shore,
Tipp'd with the silver sparkles of the moon.
The breaking waves play'd low upon the beach
Their constant music, but the air beside
Was still as starlight, and the Saviour's voice,
In its rich cadences unearthly sweet,
Seem'd like some just-born harmony in the air,
Waked by the power of wisdom. On a rock,
With the broad moonlight falling on his brow,
He stood and taught the people. At his feet
Lay his small scrip, and pilgrim's scallop-shell,

And staff—for they had waited by the sea
Till he came o'er from Gadarene, and pray'd
For his wont teachings as he came to land.
His hair was parted meekly on his brow,
And the long curls from off his shoulders fell,
As he lean'd forward earnestly, and still
The same calm cadence, passionless and deep—
And in his looks the same mild majesty—
And in his mien the sadness mix'd with power—
Fill'd them with love and wonder. Suddenly,
As on his words entrancedly they hung,
The crowd divided, and among them stood
JAIRUS THE RULER. With his flowing robe
Gather'd in haste about his loins, he came,
And fix'd his eyes on Jesus. Closer drew
The twelve disciples to their Master's side;
And silently the people shrunk away,
And left the haughty Ruler in the midst
Alone. A moment longer on the face
Of the meek Nazarene he kept his gaze,
And, as the twelve look'd on him, by the light
Of the clear moon they saw a glistening tear
Steal to his silver beard; and, drawing nigh
Unto the Saviour's feet, he took the hem
Of his coarse mantle, and with trembling hands
Press'd it upon his lips, and murmur'd low,
"*Master! my daughter!*"— * * * * * *

* * * * * * The same silvery light,
That shone upon the lone rock by the sea,
Slept on the Ruler's lofty capitals,
As at the door he stood, and welcomed in
Jesus and his disciples. All was still.
The echoing vestibule gave back the slide
Of their loose sandals, and the arrowy beam
Of moonlight, slanting to the marble floor,
Lay like a spell of silence in the rooms,
As Jairus led them on. With hushing steps
He trod the winding stair; but ere he touch'd
The latchet, from within a whisper came,
"*Trouble the Master not—for she is dead!*"
And his faint hand fell nerveless at his side,
And his steps falter'd, and his broken voice
Choked in its utterance;—but a gentle hand
Was laid upon his arm, and in his ear
The Saviour's voice sank thrillingly and low,
"*She is not dead—but sleepeth.*"

They pass'd in.
The spice-lamps in the alabaster urns
Burn'd dimly, and the white and fragrant smoke
Curl'd indolently on the chamber walls.
The silken curtains slumber'd in their folds—
Not even a tassel stirring in the air—

And as the Saviour stood beside the bed,
And pray'd inaudibly, the Ruler heard
The quickening division of his breath
As he grew earnest inwardly. There came
A gradual brightness o'er his calm, sad face;
And, drawing nearer to the bed, he moved
The silken curtains silently apart,
And look'd upon the maiden.

Like a form
Of matchless sculpture in her sleep she lay—
The linen vesture folded on her breast,
And over it her white transparent hands,
The blood still rosy in their tapering nails.
A line of pearl ran through her parted lips,
And in her nostrils, spiritually thin,
The breathing curve was mockingly like life;
And round beneath the faintly tinted skin
Ran the light branches of the azure veins;
And on her cheek the jet lash overlay,
Matching the arches pencill'd on her brow.
Her hair had been unbound, and falling loose
Upon her pillow, hid her small round ears
In curls of glossy blackness, and about
Her polish'd neck, scarce touching it, they hung,
Like airy shadows floating as they slept.
'Twas heavenly beautiful. The Saviour raised

Her hand from off her bosom, and spread out
The snowy fingers in his palm, and said,
"*Maiden! Arise!*"—and suddenly a flush
Shot o'er her forehead, and along her lips
And through her cheek the rallied color ran;
And the still outline of her graceful form
Stirr'd in the linen vesture; and she clasp'd
The Saviour's hand, and fixing her dark eyes
Full on his beaming countenance—AROSE!

The Leper.

"Room for the leper! Room!" And, as he came,
The cry pass'd on—"Room for the leper! Room!"
Sunrise was slanting on the city gates
Rosy and beautiful, and from the hills
The early risen poor were coming in,
Duly and cheerfully to their toil, and up
Rose the sharp hammer's clink, and the far hum
Of moving wheels and multitudes astir,
And all that in a city murmur swells—
Unheard but by the watcher's weary ear,
Aching with night's dull silence, or the sick
Hailing the welcome light and sounds that chase
The death-like images of the dark away.
"Room for the leper!" And aside they stood—
Matron, and child, and pitiless manhood—all
Who met him on his way—and let him pass.
And onward through the open gate he came,
A leper with the ashes on his brow,
Sackcloth about his loins, and on his lip
A covering, stepping painfully and slow,

And with a difficult utterance, like one
Whose heart is with an iron nerve put down,
Crying, "Unclean! Unclean!"

'Twas now the first
Of the Judean autumn, and the leaves,
Whose shadows lay so still upon his path,
Had put their beauty forth beneath the eye
Of Judah's loftiest noble. He was young,
And eminently beautiful, and life
Mantled in eloquent fulness on his lip,
And sparkled in his glance; and in his mien
There was a gracious pride that every eye
Follow'd with benisons—and this was he!
With the soft airs of summer there had come
A torpor on his frame, which not the speed
Of his best barb, nor music, nor the blast
Of the bold huntsman's horn, nor aught that stirs
The spirit to its bent, might drive away.
The blood beat not as wont within his veins;
Dimness crept o'er his eye; a drowsy sloth
Fetter'd his limbs like palsy, and his mien,
With all its loftiness, seem'd struck with eld.
Even his voice was changed—a languid moan
Taking the place of the clear silver key;
And brain and sense grew faint, as if the light
And very air were steep'd in sluggishness.

He strove with it awhile, as manhood will,
Ever too proud for weakness, till the rein
Slacken'd within his grasp, and in its poise
The arrowy jereed like an aspen shook.
Day after day, he lay as if in sleep.
His skin grew dry and bloodless, and white scales,
Circled with livid purple, cover'd him.
And then his nails grew black, and fell away
From the dull flesh about them, and the hues
Deepen'd beneath the hard unmoisten'd scales,
And from their edges grew the rank white hair,
—And Helon was a leper!

Day was breaking,
When at the altar of the temple stood
The holy priest of God. The incense lamp
Burn'd with a struggling light, and a low chant
Swell'd through the hollow arches of the roof
Like an articulate wail, and there, alone,
Wasted to ghastly thinness, Helon knelt.
The echoes of the melancholy strain
Died in the distant aisles, and he rose up,
Struggling with weakness, and bow'd down his head
Unto the sprinkled ashes, and put off
His costly raiment for the leper's garb;
And with the sackcloth round him, and his lip

Hid in a loathsome covering, stood still,
Waiting to hear his doom :—

Depart! depart, O child
Of Israel, from the temple of thy God!
For He has smote thee with his chastening rod;
And to the desert-wild,
From all thou lov'st, away thy feet must flee,
That from thy plague His people may be free.

Depart! and come not near
The busy mart, the crowded city, more;
Nor set thy foot a human threshold o'er;
And stay thou not to hear
Voices that call thee in the way; and fly
From all who in the wilderness pass by.

Wet not thy burning lip
In streams that to a human dwelling glide;
Nor rest thee where the covert fountains hide;
Nor kneel thee down to dip
The water where the pilgrim bends to drink,
By desert well or river's grassy brink;

And pass thou not between
The weary traveller and the cooling breeze;
And lie not down to sleep beneath the trees

Where human tracks are seen ;
Nor milk the goat that browseth on the plain,
Nor pluck the standing corn, or yellow grain.

And now depart ! and when
Thy heart is heavy, and thine eyes are dim,
Lift up thy prayer beseechingly to Him
Who, from the tribes of men,
Selected thee to feel His chastening rod.
Depart ! O leper ! and forget not God !

And he went forth—alone ! not one of all
The many whom he loved, nor she whose name
Was woven in the fibres of the heart
Breaking within him now, to come and speak
Comfort unto him. Yea—he went his way,
Sick, and heart-broken, and alone—to die !
For God had cursed the leper !

It was noon,
And Helon knelt beside a stagnant pool
In the lone wilderness, and bathed his brow,
Hot with the burning leprosy, and touch'd
The loathsome water to his fever'd lips,
Praying that he might be so blest—to die !
Footsteps approach'd, and, with no strength to flee,
He drew the covering closer on his lip,

Crying, "Unclean! unclean!" and in the folds
Of the coarse sackcloth shrouding up his face,
He fell upon the earth till they should pass.
Nearer the Stranger came, and bending o'er
The leper's prostrate form, pronounced his name—
"Helon!" The voice was like the master-tone
Of a rich instrument—most strangely sweet;
And the dull pulses of disease awoke,
And for a moment beat beneath the hot
And leprous scales with a restoring thrill.
"Helon! arise!" and he forgot his curse,
And rose and stood before Him.

Love and awe
Mingled in the regard of Helon's eye
As he beheld the stranger. He was not
In costly raiment clad, nor on his brow
The symbol of a princely lineage wore;
No followers at His back, nor in His hand
Buckler, or sword, or spear,—yet in his mien
Command sat throned serene, and if He smiled,
A kingly condescension graced His lips,
The lion would have crouch'd to in his lair.
His garb was simple, and His sandals worn;
His stature modell'd with a perfect grace;
His countenance the impress of a God,
Touch'd with the opening innocence of a child;

His eye was blue and calm, as is the sky
In the serenest noon; His hair unshorn
Fell to His shoulders; and His curling beard
The fulness of perfected manhood bore.
He look'd on Helon earnestly awhile,
As if His heart were moved, and, stooping down,
He took a little water in His hand
And laid it on his brow, and said, "Be clean!"
And lo! the scales fell from him, and his blood
Coursed with delicious coolness through his veins,
And his dry palms grew moist, and on his brow
The dewy softness of an infant's stole.
His leprosy was cleansed, and he fell down
Prostrate at Jesus' feet and worshipp'd him.

David's Grief for his Child.

'Twas daybreak, and the fingers of the dawn
Drew the night's curtain, and touch'd silently
The eyelids of the king. And David woke,
And robed himself, and pray'd. The inmates, now,
Of the vast palace were astir, and feet
Glided along the tesselated floors
With a pervading murmur, and the fount
Whose music had been all the night unheard,
Play'd as if light had made it audible;
And each one, waking, bless'd it unaware.
The fragrant strife of sunshine with the morn
Sweeten'd the air to ecstasy! and now
The king's wont was to lie upon his couch
Beneath the sky-roof of the inner court,
And, shut in from the world, but not from heaven,
Play with his loved son by the fountain's lip;
For, with idolatry confess'd alone
To the rapt wires of his reproofless harp,
He loved the child of Bathsheba. And when
The golden selvedge of his robe was heard

Sweeping the marble pavement, from within
Broke forth a child's laugh suddenly, and words—
Articulate, perhaps, to *his* heart only—
Pleading to come to him. They brought the boy—
An infant cherub, leaping as if used
To hover with that motion upon wings,
And marvellously beautiful! His brow
Had the inspired up-lift of the king's,
And kingly was his infantine regard;
But his ripe mouth was of the ravishing mould
Of Bathsheba's—the hue and type of love,
Rosy and passionate—and oh, the moist
Unfathomable blue of his large eyes
Gave out its light as twilight shows a star,
And drew the heart of the beholder in!—
And this was like his mother.

David's lips
Moved with unutter'd blessings, and awhile
He closed the lids upon his moisten'd eyes,
And, with the round cheek of the nestling boy
Press'd to his bosom, sat as if afraid
That but the lifting of his lids might jar
His heart's cup from its fulness. Unobserved,
A servant of the outer court had knelt
Waiting before him; and a cloud the while
Had rapidly spread o'er the summer heaven;

And, as the chill of the withdrawing sun
Fell on the king, he lifted up his eyes
And frown'd upon the servant—for that hour
Was hallow'd to his heart and his fair child,
And none might seek him. And the king arose,
And with a troubled countenance look'd up
To the fast-gathering darkness ; and, behold,
The servant bow'd himself to earth, and said,
" Nathan the prophet cometh from the Lord !"
And David's lips grew white, and with a clasp
Which wrung a murmur from the frighted child,
He drew him to his breast, and cover'd him
With the long foldings of his robe, and said,
" I will come forth. Go now !" And lingeringly,
With kisses on the fair uplifted brow,
And mingled words of tenderness and prayer
Breaking in tremulous accents from his lips,
He gave to them the child, and bow'd his head
Upon his breast with agony. And so,
To hear the errand of the man of God,
He fearfully went forth.

* * * * * * * * *

It was the morning of the seventh day.
A hush was in the palace, for all eyes
Had woke before the morn ; and they who drew
The curtains to let in the welcome light,
Moved in their chambers with unslipper'd feet,

And listen'd breathlessly. And still no stir!
The servants who kept watch without the door
Sat motionless; the purple casement-shades
From the low windows had been roll'd away,
To give the child air: and the flickering light
That, all the night, within the spacious court,
Had drawn the watcher's eyes to one spot only,
Paled with the sunrise and fled in.

And hush'd
With more than stillness was the room where lay
The king's son on his mother's breast. His locks
Slept at the lips of Bathsheba unstirr'd—
So fearfully, with heart and pulse kept down,
She watch'd his breathless slumber. The low moan
That from his lips all night broke fitfully,
Had silenced with the daybreak; and a smile—
Or something that would fain have been a smile—
Play'd in his parted mouth; and though his lids
Hid not the blue of his unconscious eyes,
His senses seem'd all peacefully asleep,
And Bathsheba in silence bless'd the morn—
That brought back hope to her! But when the king
Heard not the voice of the complaining child,
Nor breath from out the room, nor foot astir—

But morning there—so welcomeless and still—
He groan'd and turn'd upon his face. The nights
Had wasted; and the mornings come; and days
Crept through the sky, unnumber'd by the king,
Since the child sicken'd; and, without the door,
Upon the bare earth prostrate, he had lain—
Listening only to the moans that brought
Their inarticulate tidings, and the voice
Of Bathsheba, whose pity and caress,
In loving utterance all broke with tears,
Spoke as his heart would speak if he were there,
And fill'd his prayer with agony. Oh God!
To thy bright mercy-seat the way is far!
How fail the weak words while the heart keeps on!
And when the spirit, mournfully, at last,
Kneels at thy throne, how cold, how distantly
The comforting of friends falls on the ear—
The anguish they would speak to, gone to Thee!

But suddenly the watchers at the door
Rose up, and they who minister'd within
Crept to the threshold and look'd earnestly
Where the king lay. And still, while Bathsheba
Held the unmoving child upon her knees,
The curtains were let down, and all came forth,
And, gathering with fearful looks apart,
Whisper'd together.

And the king arose
And gazed on them a moment, and with voice
Of quick, uncertain utterance, he ask'd,
"Is the child dead?" They answer'd, "He is dead!"
But when they look'd to see him fall again
Upon his face, and rend himself and weep—
For, while the child was sick, his agony
Would bear no comforters, and they had thought
His heartstrings with the tidings must give way—
Behold! his face grew calm, and, with his robe
Gather'd together like his kingly wont,
He silently went in.

And David came,
Robed and anointed, forth, and to the house
Of God went up to pray. And he return'd,
And they set bread before him, and he ate—
And when they marvell'd, he said, "*Wherefore mourn?*
The child is dead, and I shall go to him—
But he will not return to me."

The Sacrifice of Abraham.

MORN breaketh in the east. The purple clouds
Are putting on their gold and violet,
To look the meeter for the sun's bright coming.
Sleep is upon the waters and the wind;
And nature, from the wavy forest-leaf
To her majestic master, sleeps. As yet
There is no mist upon the deep blue sky,
And the clear dew is on the blushing bosoms
Of crimson roses in a holy rest.
How hallow'd is the hour of morning! meet—
Ay, beautifully meet—for the pure prayer.
The patriarch standeth at his tented door,
With his white locks uncover'd. 'Tis his wont
To gaze upon that gorgeous Orient;
And at that hour the awful majesty
Of man who talketh often with his God,
Is wont to come again, and clothe his brow
As at his fourscore strength. But now, he seemeth
To be forgetful of his vigorous frame,
And boweth to his staff as at the hour

Of noontide sultriness. And that bright sun—
He looketh at its pencill'd messengers,
Coming in golden raiment, as if all
Were but a graven scroll of fearfulness.
Ah, he is waiting till it herald in
The hour to sacrifice his much-loved son!

Light poureth on the world. And Sarah stands
Watching the steps of Abraham and her child
Along the dewy sides of the far hills,
And praying that her sunny boy faint not.
Would she have watch'd their path so silently,
If she had known that he was going up,
E'en in his fair-hair'd beauty, to be slain
As a white lamb for sacrifice? They trod
Together onward, patriarch and child—
The bright sun throwing back the old man's shade
In straight and fair proportions, as of one
Whose years were freshly number'd. He stood up,
Tall in his vigorous strength; and, like a tree
Rooted in Lebanon, his frame bent not.
His thin white hairs had yielded to the wind,
And left his brow uncover'd; and his face,
Impress'd with the stern majesty of grief
Nerved to a solemn duty, now stood forth
Like a rent rock, submissive, yet sublime.
But the young boy--he of the laughing eye

And ruby lip—the pride of life was on him.
He seem'd to drink the morning. Sun and dew,
And the aroma of the spicy trees,
And all that giveth the delicious East
Its fitness for an Eden, stole like light
Into his spirit, ravishing his thoughts
With love and beauty. Every thing he met,
Buoyant or beautiful, the lightest wing
Of bird or insect, or the palest dye
Of the fresh flowers, won him from his path;
And joyously broke forth his tiny shout,
As he flung back his silken hair, and sprung
Away to some green spot or clustering vine,
To pluck his infant trophies. Every tree
And fragrant shrub was a new hiding-place;
And he would crouch till the old man came by,
Then bound before him with his childish laugh,
Stealing a look behind him playfully,
To see if he had made his father smile.
The sun rode on in heaven. The dew stole up
From the fresh daughters of the earth, and hea
Came like a sleep upon the delicate leaves,
And bent them with the blossoms to their dreams
Still trod the patriarch on, with that same step,
Firm and unfaltering; turning not aside
To seek the olive shades, or lave their lips
In the sweet waters of the Syrian wells,

Whose gush hath so much music. Weariness
Stole on the gentle boy, and he forgot
To toss his sunny hair from off his brow,
And spring for the fresh flowers and light wings
As in the early morning; but he kept
Close by his father's side, and bent his head
Upon his bosom like a drooping bud,
Lifting it not, save now and then to steal
A look up to the face whose sternness awed
His childishness to silence.

It was noon—
And Abraham on Moriah bow'd himself,
And buried up his face, and pray'd for strength.
He could not look upon his son, and pray;
But, with his hand upon the clustering curls
Of the fair, kneeling boy, he pray'd that God
Would nerve him for that hour. Oh! man was made
For the stern conflict. In a mother's love
There is more tenderness; the thousand chords,
Woven with every fibre of her heart,
Complain, like delicate harp-strings, at a breath;
But love in man is one deep principle,
Which, like a root grown in a rifted rock,
Abides the tempest. He rose up, and laid
The wood upon the altar. All was done.

He stood a moment—and a deep, quick flush
Pass'd o'er his countenance ; and then he nerved
His spirit with a bitter strength, and spoke—
" Isaac ! my only son !"—The boy look'd up,
And Abraham turn'd his face away, and wept.
" Where is the lamb, my father ?"—Oh the tones,
The sweet, the thrilling music of a child !—
How it doth agonize at such an hour !—
It was the last deep struggle. Abraham held
His loved, his beautiful, his only son,
And lifted up his arm, and call'd on God—
And lo ! God's angel stay'd him—and he fell
Upon his face, and wept.

The Shunammite.

It was a sultry day of summer-time.
The sun pour'd down upon the ripen'd grain
With quivering heat, and the suspended leaves
Hung motionless. The cattle on the hills
Stood still, and the divided flock were all
Laying their nostrils to the cooling roots,
And the sky look'd like silver, and it seem'd
As if the air had fainted, and the pulse
Of nature had run down, and ceased to beat.

"Haste thee, my child!" the Syrian mother said,
"Thy father is athirst"—and, from the depths
Of the cool well under the leaning tree,
She drew refreshing water, and with thoughts
Of God's sweet goodness stirring at her heart,
She bless'd her beautiful boy, and to his way
Committed him. And he went lightly on,
With his soft hands press'd closely to the cool
Stone vessel, and his little naked feet
Lifted with watchful care; and o'er the hills,

And through the light green hollows where the lambs
Go for the tender grass, he kept his way,
Wiling its distance with his simple thoughts,
Till, in the wilderness of sheaves, with brows
Throbbing with heat, he set his burden down.

Childhood is restless ever, and the boy
Stay'd not within the shadow of the tree,
But with a joyous industry went forth
Into the reapers' places, and bound up
His tiny sheaves, and plaited cunningly
The pliant withs out of the shining straw—
Cheering their labor on, till they forgot
The heat and weariness of their stooping toil
In the beguiling of his playful mirth.
Presently he was silent, and his eye
Closed as with dizzy pain, and with his hand
Press'd hard upon his forehead, and his breast
Heaving with the suppression of a cry,
He utter'd a faint murmur, and fell back
Upon the loosen'd sheaf, insensible.

They bore him to his mother, and he lay
Upon her knees till noon—and then he died!
She had watch'd every breath, and kept her hand
Soft on his forehead, and gazed in upon

The dreamy languor of his listless eye,
And she had laid back all his sunny curls
And kiss'd his delicate lip, and lifted him
Into her bosom, till her heart grew strong—
His beauty was so unlike death! She lean'd
Over him now, that she might catch the low
Sweet music of his breath, that she had learn'd
To love when he was slumbering at her side
In his unconscious infancy—
"—So still!
'Tis a soft sleep! How beautiful he lies,
With his fair forehead, and the rosy veins
Playing so freshly in his sunny cheek!
How could they say that he would die! Oh God!
I could not lose him! I have treasured all
His childhood in my heart, and even now,
As he has slept, my memory has been there,
Counting like treasures all his winning ways—
His unforgotten sweetness:—
"—Yet so still!—
How like this breathless slumber is to death!
I could believe that in that bosom now
There were no pulse—it beats so languidly!
I cannot see it stir; but his red lip!
Death would not be so very beautiful!
And that half smile—would death have left *that* there?

—And should I not have felt that he would die?
And have I not wept over him?—and pray'd
Morning and night for him? and *could* he die?
—No—God will keep him! He will be my pride
Many long years to come, and his fair hair
Will darken like his father's, and his eye
Be of a deeper blue when he is grown;
And he will be so tall, and I shall look
With such a pride upon him!—*He* to die!"
And the fond mother lifted his soft curls,
And smiled, as if 'twere mockery to think
That such fair things could perish—
—Suddenly
Her hand shrunk from him, and the color fled
From her fix'd lip, and her supporting knees
Were shook beneath her child. Her hand had touch'd
His forehead, as she dallied with his hair—
And it was cold—like clay! Slow, very slow,
Came the misgiving that her child was dead.
She sat a moment, and her eyes were closed
In a dumb prayer for strength, and then she took
His little hand and press'd it earnestly—
And put her lip to his—and look'd again
Fearfully on him—and, then bending low,
She whisper'd in his ear, "My son!—my son!"
And as the echo died, and not a sound

Broke on the stillness, and he lay there still—
Motionless on her knee—the truth *would* come!
And with a sharp, quick cry, as if her heart
Were crush'd, she lifted him and held him close
Into her bosom—with a mother's thought—
As if death had no power to touch him there!
* * * * * * * * *
The man of God came forth, and led the child
Unto his mother, and went on his way.
And he was there—her beautiful—her own—
Living and smiling on her—with his arms
Folded about her neck, and his warm breath
Breathing upon her lips, and in her ear
The music of his gentle voice once more!

Jephthah's Daughter.

She stood before her father's gorgeous tent,
To listen for his coming. Her loose hair
Was resting on her shoulders, like a cloud
Floating around a statue, and the wind,
Just swaying her light robe, reveal'd a shape
Praxiteles might worship. She had clasp'd
Her hands upon her bosom, and had raised
Her beautiful, dark, Jewish eyes to heaven,
Till the long lashes lay upon her brow.
Her lip was slightly parted, like the cleft
Of a pomegranate blossom; and her neck,
Just where the cheek was melting to its curve
With the unearthly beauty sometimes there,
Was shaded, as if light had fallen off,
Its surface was so polish'd. She was stilling
Her light, quick breath, to hear; and the white rose
Scarce moved upon her bosom, as it swell'd,
Like nothing but a lovely wave of light,
To meet the arching of her queenly neck.

Her countenance was radiant with love.
She look'd like one to die for it—a being
Whose whole existence was the pouring out
Of rich and deep affections. I have thought
A brother's and a sister's love were much;
I know a brother's is—for I have been
A sister's idol—and I know how full
The heart may be of tenderness to her!
But the affection of a delicate child
For a fond father, gushing, as it does,
With the sweet springs of life, and pouring on,
Through all earth's changes, like a river's course—
Chasten'd with reverence, and made more pure
By the world's discipline of light and shade—
'Tis deeper—holier.
The wind bore on
The leaden tramp of thousands. Clarion notes
Rang sharply on the ear at intervals;
And the low, mingled din of mighty hosts
Returning from the battle, pour'd from far,
Like the deep murmur of a restless sea.
They came, as earthly conquerors always come,
With blood and splendor, revelry and wo.
The stately horse treads proudly—he hath trod
The brow of death, as well. The chariot-wheels
Of warriors roll magnificently on—
Their weight hath crush'd the fallen. *Man* is there—

Majestic, lordly man—with his sublime
And elevated brow, and godlike frame;
Lifting his crest in triumph—for his heel
Hath trod the dying like a wine-press down!

The mighty Jephthah led his warriors on
Through Mizpeh's streets. His helm was proudly set,
And his stern lip curl'd slightly, as if praise
Were for the hero's scorn. His step was firm,
But free as India's leopard; and his mail,
Whose shekels none in Israel might bear,
Was like a cedar's tassel on his frame.
His crest was Judah's kingliest; and the look
Of his dark, lofty eye, and bended brow,
Might quell the lion. He led on; but thoughts
Seem'd gathering round which troubled him. The veins
Grew visible upon his swarthy brow,
And his proud lip was press'd as if with pain.
He trod less firmly; and his restless eye
Glanced forward frequently, as if some ill
He dared not meet, were there. His home was near;
And men were thronging, with that strange delight
They have in human passions, to observe
The struggle of his feelings with his pride

He gazed intensely forward. The tall firs
Before his tent were motionless. The leaves
Of the sweet aloe, and the clustering vines
Which half conceal'd his threshold, met his eye,
Unchanged and beautiful; and one by one,
The balsam, with its sweet-distilling stems,
And the Circassian rose, and all the crowd
Of silent and familiar things stole up,
Like the recover'd passages of dreams.
He strode on rapidly. A moment more,
And he had reach'd his home; when lo! there sprang
One with a bounding footstep, and a brow
Of light, to meet him. Oh how beautiful!—
Her dark eye flashing like a sun-lit gem—
And her luxuriant hair!—'twas like the sweep
Of a swift wing in visions. He stood still,
As if the sight had wither'd him. She threw
Her arms about his neck—he heeded not.
She call'd him "Father"—but he answer'd not.
She stood and gazed upon him. Was he wroth?
There was no anger in that blood-shot eye.
Had sickness seized him? She unclasp'd his helm,
And laid her white hand gently on his brow,
And the large veins felt stiff and hard, like cords.
The touch aroused him. He raised up his hands,
And spoke the name of God, in agony.

She knew that he was stricken, then; and rush'd
Again into his arms; and, with a flood
Of tears she could not bridle, sobb'd a prayer
That he would breathe his agony in words.
He told her—and a momentary flush
Shot o'er her countenance; and then the soul
Of Jephthah's daughter waken'd; and she stood
Calmly and nobly up, and said 'twas well—
And she would die. * * * * *
The sun had well nigh set.
The fire was on the altar; and the priest
Of the High God was there. A pallid man
Was stretching out his trembling hands to heaven,
As if he would have pray'd, but had no words—
And she who was to die, the calmest one
In Israel at that hour, stood up alone,
And waited for the sun to set. Her face
Was pale, but very beautiful—her lip
Had a more delicate outline, and the tint
Was deeper; but her countenance was like
The majesty of angels.
The sun set—
And she was dead—but not by violence

Absalom.

THE waters slept. Night's silvery veil hung low
On Jordan's bosom, and the eddies curl'd
Their glassy rings beneath it, like the still,
Unbroken beating of the sleeper's pulse.
The reeds bent down the stream; the willow leaves,
With a soft cheek upon the lulling tide,
Forgot the lifting winds; and the long stems,
Whose flowers the water, like a gentle nurse,
Bears on its bosom, quietly gave way,
And lean'd, in graceful attitudes, to rest.
How strikingly the course of nature tells,
By its light heed of human suffering,
That it was fashion'd for a happier world!
  King David's limbs were weary. He had fled
From far Jerusalem; and now he stood,
With his faint people, for a little rest
Upon the shore of Jordan. The light wind
Of morn was stirring, and he bared his brow
To its refreshing breath; for he had worn

The mourner's covering, and he had not felt
That he could see his people until now.
They gather'd round him on the fresh green bank,
And spoke their kindly words; and, as the sun
Rose up in heaven, he knelt among them there,
And bow'd his head upon his hands to pray.
Oh! when the heart is full—when bitter thoughts
Come crowding thickly up for utterance,
And the poor common words of courtesy
Are such a very mockery—how much
The bursting heart may pour itself in prayer!
He pray'd for Israel—and his voice went up
Strongly and fervently. He pray'd for those
Whose love had been his shield—and his deep tones
Grew tremulous. But, oh! for Absalom—
For his estranged, misguided Absalom—
The proud, bright being, who had burst away
In all his princely beauty, to defy
The heart that cherish'd him—for him he pour'd,
In agony that would not be controll'd,
Strong supplication, and forgave him there,
Before his God, for his deep sinfulness.
* * * * * * * * *

The pall was settled. He who slept beneath
Was straighten'd for the grave; and, as the folds
Sunk to the still proportions, they betray'd

The matchless symmetry of Absalom.
His hair was yet unshorn, and silken curls
Were floating round the tassels as they sway'd
To the admitted air, as glossy now
As when, in hours of gentle dalliance, bathing
The snowy fingers of Judea's daughters.
His helm was at his feet: his banner, soil'd
With trailing through Jerusalem, was laid,
Reversed, beside him: and the jewell'd hilt,
Whose diamonds lit the passage of his blade,
Rested, like mockery, on his cover'd brow.
The soldiers of the king trod to and fro,
Clad in the garb of battle; and their chief,
The mighty Joab, stood beside the bier,
And gazed upon the dark pall steadfastly,
As if he fear'd the slumberer might stir.
A slow step startled him. He grasp'd his blade
As if a trumpet rang; but the bent form
Of David enter'd, and he gave command,
In a low tone, to his few followers,
And left him with his dead. The king stood still
Till the last echo died; then, throwing off
The sackcloth from his brow, and laying back
The pall from the still features of his child,
He bow'd his head upon him, and broke forth
In the resistless eloquence of wo:

"Alas! my noble boy! that thou shouldst die!
  Thou, who wert made so beautifully fair!
That death should settle in thy glorious eye,
  And leave his stillness in this clustering hair!
How could he mark thee for the silent tomb!
    My proud boy, Absalom!

"Cold is thy brow, my son! and I am chill,
  As to my bosom I have tried to press thee!
How was I wont to feel my pulses thrill,
  Like a rich harp-string, yearning to caress thee,
And hear thy sweet '*my father!*' from these dumb
    And cold lips, Absalom!

"But death is on thee. I shall hear the gush
  Of music, and the voices of the young;
And life will pass me in the mantling blush,
  And the dark tresses to the soft winds flung;—
But thou no more, with thy sweet voice, shalt come
    To meet me, Absalom!

"And oh! when I am stricken, and my heart,
  Like a bruised reed, is waiting to be broken,
How will its love for thee, as I depart,
  Yearn for thine ear to drink its last deep token!
It were so sweet, amid death's gathering gloom,
    To see thee, Absalom!

"And now, farewell! 'Tis hard to give thee up,
With death so like a gentle slumber on thee;—
And thy dark sin!—Oh! I could drink the cup,
If from this wo its bitterness had won thee.
May God have call'd thee, like a wanderer, home,
My lost boy Absalom!"

He cover'd up his face, and bow'd himself
A moment on his child: then, giving him
A look of melting tenderness, ne clasp'd
His hands convulsively, as if in prayer;
And, as if strength were given him of God,
He rose up calmly, and composed the pall
Firmly and decently—and left him there—
As if his rest had been a breathing sleep.

Christ's Entrance into Jerusalem.

He sat upon the "ass's foal" and rode
Toward Jerusalem. Beside him walk'd,
Closely and silently, the faithful twelve,
And on before him went a multitude
Shouting Hosannas, and with eager hands
Strewing their garments thickly in his way.
Th' unbroken foal beneath him gently stepp'd,
Tame as its patient dam; and as the song
Of "welcome to the Son of David" burst
Forth from a thousand children, and the leaves
Of the waved branches touch'd its silken ears,
It turn'd its wild eye for a moment back,
And then, subdued by an invisible hand,
Meekly trode onward with its slender feet.

The dew's last sparkle from the grass had gone
As he rode up Mount Olivet. The woods
Threw their cool shadows freshly to the west,
And the light foal, with quick and toiling step,
And head bent low, kept its unslacken'd way

Till its soft mane was lifted by the wind
Sent o'er the mount from Jordan. As he reach'd
The summit's breezy pitch, the Saviour raised
His calm blue eye—there stood Jerusalem!
Eagerly he bent forward, and beneath
His mantle's passive folds, a bolder line
Than the wont slightness of his perfect limbs
Betray'd the swelling fulness of his heart.
There stood Jerusalem! How fair she look'd—
The silver sun on all her palaces,
And her fair daughters 'mid the golden spires
Tending their terrace flowers, and Kedron's stream
Lacing the meadows with its silver band,
And wreathing its mist-mantle on the sky
With the morn's exhalations. There she stood—
Jerusalem—the city of his love,
Chosen from all the earth; Jerusalem—
That knew him not—and had rejected him;
Jerusalem—for whom he came to die!
The shouts redoubled from a thousand lips
At the fair sight; the children leap'd and sang
Louder Hosannas; the clear air was fill'd
With odor from the trampled olive-leaves—
But "Jesus wept." The loved disciple saw
His Master's tears, and closer to his side
He came with yearning looks, and on his neck
The Saviour leant with heavenly tenderness,

And mourn'd—" How oft, Jerusalem ! would I
Have gather'd you, as gathereth a hen
Her brood beneath her wings—but ye would not !"

He thought not of the death that he should die—
He thought not of the thorns he knew must pierce
His forehead—of the buffet on the cheek—
The scourge, the mocking homage, the foul scorn !—
Gethsemane stood out beneath his eye
Clear in the morning sun, and there, he knew,
While they who " could not watch with him one hour"
Were sleeping, he should sweat great drops of blood,
Praying the " cup might pass." And Golgotha
Stood bare and desert by the city wall,
And in its midst, to his prophetic eye,
Rose the rough cross, and its keen agonies
Were number'd all—the nails were in his feet—
Th' insulting sponge was pressing on his lips—
The blood and water gushing from his side—
The dizzy faintness swimming in his brain—
And, while his own disciples fled in fear,
A world's death-agonies all mix'd in his !
Ay !—he forgot all this. He only saw
Jerusalem,—the chos'n—the loved—the lost !

He only felt that for her sake his life
Was vainly giv'n, and, in his pitying love,
The sufferings that would clothe the Heavens in
black,
Were quite forgotten. Was there ever love,
In earth or heaven, equal unto this?

Baptism of Christ.

It was a green spot in the wilderness,
Touch'd by the river Jordan. The dark pine
Never had dropp'd its tassels on the moss
Tufting the leaning bank, nor on the grass
Of the broad circle stretching evenly
To the straight larches, had a heavier foot
Than the wild heron's trodden. Softly in
Through a long aisle of willows, dim and cool,
Stole the clear waters with their muffled feet,
And, hushing as they spread into the light,
Circled the edges of the pebbled tank
Slowly, then rippled through the woods away.
Hither had come th' Apostle of the wild,
Winding the river's course. 'Twas near the flush
Of eve, and, with a multitude around,
Who from the cities had come out to hear,
He stood breast-high amid the running stream,
Baptizing as the Spirit gave him power.
His simple raiment was of camel's hair,
A leathern girdle close about his loins,

His beard unshorn, and for his daily meat
The locust and wild honey of the wood—
But like the face of Moses on the mount
Shone his rapt countenance, and in his eye
Burn'd the mild fire of love—and as he spoke
The ear lean'd to him, and persuasion swift
To the chain'd spirit of the listener stole

Silent upon the green and sloping bank
The people sat, and while the leaves were shook
With the birds dropping early to their nests.
And the gray eve came on, within their hearts
They mused if he were Christ. The rippling
stream
Still turn'd its silver courses from his breast
As he divined their thought. "I but baptize,"
He said, "with water; but there cometh One,
The latchet of whose shoes I may not dare
E'en to unloose. He will baptize with fire
And with the Holy Ghost." And lo! while yet
The words were on his lips, he raised his eyes
And on the bank stood Jesus. He had laid
His raiment off, and with his loins alone
Girt with a mantle, and his perfect limbs,
In their angelic slightness, meek and bare,
He waited to go in. But John forbade,
And hurried to his feet and stay'd him there,

And said, " Nay, Master ! I have need of *thine*,
Not thou of *mine !*" And Jesus, with a smile
Of heavenly sadness, met his earnest looks,
And answer'd, " Suffer it to be so now ;
For thus it doth become me to fulfil
All righteousness." And, leaning to the stream,
He took around him the Apostle's arm,
And drew him gently to the midst. The wood
Was thick with the dim twilight as they came
Up from the water With his clasped hands
Laid on his breast, th' Apostle silently
Follow'd his master's steps—when lo ! a light,
Bright as the tenfold glory of the sun,
Yet lambent as the softly burning stars,
Envelop'd them, and from the heavens away
Parted the dim blue ether like a veil ;
And as a voice, fearful exceedingly,
Broke from the midst, " THIS IS MY MUCH LOVED SON
IN WHOM I AM WELL PLEASED," a snow-white dove,
Floating upon its wings, descended through ;
And shedding a swift music from its plumes,
Circled, and flutter'd to the Saviour's breast.

Scene in Gethsemane.

THE moon was shining yet. The Orient's brow,
Set with the morning-star, was not yet dim ;
And the deep silence which subdues the breath
Like a strong feeling, hung upon the world
As sleep upon the pulses of a child.
'Twas the last watch of night. Gethsemane,
With its bathed leaves of silver, seem'd dissolved
In visible stillness ; and as Jesus' voice,
With its bewildering sweetness, met the ear
Of his disciples, it vibrated on
Like the first whisper in a silent world.
They came on slowly. Heaviness oppress'd
The Saviour's heart, and when the kindnesses
Of his deep love were pour'd, he felt the need
Of near communion, for his gift of strength
Was wasted by the spirit's weariness.
He left them there, and went a little on,
And in the depth of that hush'd silentness,
Alone with God, he fell upon his face,
And as his heart was broken with the rush

Of his surpassing agony, and death,
Wrung to him from a dying universe,
Was mightier than the Son of man could bear,
He gave his sorrows way—and in the deep
Prostration of his soul, breathed out the prayer,
" Father, if it be possible with thee,
Let this cup pass from me." Oh, how a word,
Like the forced drop before the fountain breaks,
Stilleth the press of human agony!
The Saviour felt its quiet in his soul;
And though his strength was weakness, and the light
Which led him on till now was sorely dim,
He breathed a new submission—" Not my will,
But thine be done, oh Father!" As he spoke,
Voices were heard in heaven, and music stole
Out from the chambers of the vaulted sky
As if the stars were swept like instruments.
No cloud was visible, but radiant wings
Were coming with a silvery rush to earth,
And as the Saviour rose, a glorious one,
With an illumined forehead, and the light
Whose fountain is the mystery of God,
Encalm'd within his eye, bow'd down to him,
And nerved him with a ministry of strength.
It was enough—and with his godlike brow
Re-written of his Father's messenger,

With meekness, whose divinity is more
Than power and glory, he return'd again
To his disciples, and awaked their sleep,
For "he that should betray him was at hand."

The Widow of Nain.

THE Roman sentinel stood helm'd and tall
Beside the gate of Nain. The busy tread
Of comers to the city mart was done,
For it was almost noon, and a dead heat
Quiver'd upon the fine and sleeping dust,
And the cold snake crept panting from the wall,
And bask'd his scaly circles in the sun.
Upon his spear the soldier lean'd, and kept
His idle watch, and, as his drowsy dream
Was broken by the solitary foot
Of some poor mendicant, he raised his head
To curse him for a tributary Jew,
And slumberously dozed on.

'Twas now high noon.
The dull, low murmur of a funeral
Went through the city—the sad sound of feet
Unmix'd with voices—and the sentinel
Shook off his slumber, and gazed earnestly
Up the wide streets along whose paved way

The silent throng crept slowly. They came on,
Bearing a body heavily on its bier,
And by the crowd that in the burning sun,
Walk'd with forgetful sadness, 'twas of one
Mourn'd with uncommon sorrow. The broad gate
Swung on its hinges, and the Roman bent
His spear-point downwards as the bearers pass'd,
Bending beneath their burden. There was one—
Only one mourner. Close behind the bier,
Crumpling the pall up in her wither'd hands,
Follow'd an aged woman. Her short steps
Falter'd with weakness, and a broken moan
Fell from her lips, thicken'd convulsively
As her heart bled afresh. The pitying crowd
Follow'd apart, but no one spoke to her.
She had no kinsmen. She had lived alone—
A widow with one son. He was her all—
The only tie she had in the wide world—
And he was dead. They could not comfort her.

Jesus drew near to Nain as from the gate
The funeral came forth. His lips were pale
With the noon's sultry heat. The beaded sweat
Stood thickly on his brow, and on the worn
And simple latchets of his sandals lay,
Thick, the white dust of travel. He had come
Since sunrise from Capernaum, staying not

To wet his lips by green Bethsaida's pool,
Nor wash his feet in Kishon's silver springs,
Nor turn him southward upon Tabor's side
To catch Gilboa's light and spicy breeze.
Genesareth stood cool upon the East,
Fast by the Sea of Galilee, and there
The weary traveller might bide till eve;
And on the alders of Bethulia's plains
The grapes of Palestine hung ripe and wild;
Yet turn'd he not aside, but, gazing on,
From every swelling mount he saw afar,
Amid the hills, the humble spires of Nain,
The place of his next errand; and the path
Touch'd not Bethulia, and a league away
Upon the East lay pleasant Galilee.

Forth from the city-gate the pitying crowd
Follow'd the stricken mourner. They came near
The place of burial, and, with straining hands,
Closer upon her breast she clasp'd the pall,
And with a gasping sob, quick as a child's,
And an inquiring wildness flashing through
The thin gray lashes of her fever'd eyes,
She came where Jesus stood beside the way.
He look'd upon her, and his heart was moved.
"Weep not!" he said; and as they stay'd the bier,
And at his bidding laid it at his feet,

He gently drew the pall from out her grasp,
And laid it back in silence from the dead.
With troubled wonder the mute throng drew near,
And gazed on his calm looks. A minute's space
He stood and pray'd. Then, taking the cold hand,
He said, "Arise!" And instantly the breast
Heaved in its cerements, and a sudden flush
Ran through the lines of the divided lips,
And with a murmur of his mother's name,
He trembled and sat upright in his shroud.
And, while the mourner hung upon his neck,
Jesus went calmly on his way to Nain.

Hagar in the Wilderness.

THE morning broke. Light stole upon the clouds
With a strange beauty. Earth received again
Its garment of a thousand dyes; and leaves,
And delicate blossoms, and the painted flowers,
And every thing that bendeth to the dew;
And stirreth with the daylight, lifted up
Its beauty to the breath of that sweet morn.

All things are dark to sorrow; and the light
And loveliness, and fragrant air were sad
To the dejected Hagar. The moist earth
Was pouring odors from its spicy pores,
And the young birds were singing as if life
Were a new thing to them; but oh! it came
Upon her heart like discord, and she felt
How cruelly it tries a broken heart,
To see a mirth in any thing it loves.
She stood at Abraham's tent. Her lips were press'd
Till the blood started; and the wandering veins
Of her transparent forehead were swell'd out,

As if her pride would burst them. Her dark eye
Was clear and tearless, and the light of heaven,
Which made its language legible, shot back,
From her long lashes, as it had been flame.
Her noble boy stood by her, with his hand
Clasp'd in her own, and his round, delicate feet,
Scarce train'd to balance on the tented floor,
Sandall'd for journeying. He had look'd up
Into his mother's face until he caught
The spirit there, and his young heart was swelling
Beneath his dimpled bosom, and his form
Straighten'd up proudly in his tiny wrath,
As if his light proportions would have swell'd,
Had they but match'd his spirit, to the man.

Why bends the patriarch as he cometh now
Upon his staff so wearily? His beard
Is low upon his breast, and his high brow,
So written with the converse of his God,
Beareth the swollen vein of agony.
His lip is quivering, and his wonted step
Of vigor is not there; and, though the morn
Is passing fair and beautiful, he breathes
Its freshness as it were a pestilence.
Oh! man may bear with suffering: his heart
Is a strong thing, and godlike, in the grasp
Of pain that wrings mortality; but tear

One chord affection clings to—part one tie
That binds him to a woman's delicate love—
And his great spirit yieldeth like a reed.

He gave to her the water and the bread,
But spoke no word, and trusted not himself
To look upon her face, but laid his hand
In silent blessing on the fair-hair'd boy,
And left her to her lot of loneliness

Should Hagar weep? May slighted woman turn,
And, as a vine the oak hath shaken off,
Bend lightly to her leaning trust again?
O no! by all her loveliness—by all
That makes life poetry and beauty, no!
Make her a slave; steal from her rosy cheek
By needless jealousies; let the last star
Leave her a watcher by your couch of pain;
Wrong her by petulance, suspicion, all
That makes her cup a bitterness—yet give
One evidence of love, and earth has not
An emblem of devotedness like hers.
But oh! estrange her once—it boots not how—
By wrong or silence—any thing that tells
A change has come upon your tenderness,—
And there is not a feeling out of heaven
Her pride o'ermastereth not.

She went her way with a strong step and slow—
Her press'd lip arch'd, and her clear eye undimm'd,
As if it were a diamond, and her form
Borne proudly up, as if her heart breathed through,
Her child kept on in silence, though she press'd
His hand till it was pain'd ; for he had caught,
As I have said, her spirit, and the seed
Of a stern nation had been breathed upon.

The morning pass'd, and Asia's sun rode up
In the clear heaven, and every beam was heat.
The cattle of the hills were in the shade,
And the bright plumage of the Orient lay
On beating bosoms in her spicy trees.
It was an hour of rest ! but Hagar found
No shelter in the wilderness, and on
She kept her weary way, until the boy
Hung down his head, and open'd his parch'd lips
For water ; but she could not give it him.
She laid him down beneath the sultry sky,—
For it was better than the close, hot breath
Of the thick pines,—and tried to comfort him ;
But he was sore athirst, and his blue eyes
Were dim and bloodshot, and he could not know
Why God denied him water in the wild.
She sat a little longer, and he grew
Ghastly and faint, as if he would have died.

It was too much for her. She lifted him,
And bore him further on, and laid his head
Beneath the shadow of a desert shrub,
And, shrouding up her face, she went away,
And sat to watch, where he could see her not,
Till he should die; and, watching him, she
mourn'd:—

"God stay thee in thine agony, my boy
I cannot see thee die; I cannot brook
Upon thy brow to look,
And see death settle on my cradle joy.
How have I drunk the light of thy blue eye!
And could I see thee die?

"I did not dream of this when thou wast
straying,
Like an unbound gazelle, among the flowers;
Or wiling the soft hours,
By the rich gush of water-sources playing,
Then sinking weary to thy smiling sleep,
So beautiful and deep.

"Oh no! and when I watch'd by thee the while,
And saw thy bright lip curling in thy dream,
And thought of the dark stream
In my own land of Egypt, the far Nile,

How pray'd I that my father's land might be
An heritage for thee!

"And now the grave for its cold breast hath won thee!
And thy white, delicate limbs the earth will press;
And oh! my last caress
Must feel thee cold, for a chill hand is on thee.
How can I leave my boy, so pillow'd there
Upon his clustering hair!"

She stood beside the well her God had given
To gush in that deep wilderness, and bathed
The forehead of her child until he laugh'd
In his reviving happiness, and lisp'd
His infant thought of gladness at the sight
Of the cool plashing of his mother's hand

Rizpah with her Sons,

(The day before they were hanged on Gibeah.)

"Bread for my mother!" said the voice of one
Darkening the door of Rizpah. She look'd up—
And lo! the princely countenance and mien
Of dark-brow'd Armoni. The eye of Saul—
The very voice and presence of the king—
Limb, port, and majesty,—were present there,
Mock'd like an apparition in her son.
Yet, as he stoop'd his forehead to her hand
With a kind smile, a something of his mother
Unbent the haughty arching of his lip,
And, through the darkness of the widow's heart
Trembled a nerve of tenderness that shook
Her thought of pride all suddenly to tears.

"Whence comest thou? said Rizpah.

"From the house
Of David. In his gate there stood a soldier—
This in his hand. I pluck'd it, and I said,

'A king's son takes it for his hungry mother!'
God stay the famine!"

* * * * * * As he spoke, a step,
Light as an antelope's, the threshold press'd,
And like a beam of light into the room
Enter'd Mephibosheth. What bird of heaven
Or creature of the wild—what flower of earth—
Was like this fairest of the sons of Saul!
The violet's cup was harsh to his blue eye.
Less agile was the fierce barb's fiery step.
His voice drew hearts to him. His smile was like
The incarnation of some blessed dream—
Its joyousness so sunn'd the gazer's eye!
Fair were his locks. His snowy teeth divided
A bow of Love, drawn with a scarlet thread.
His cheek was like the moist heart of the rose;
And, but for nostrils of that breathing fire
That turns the lion back, and limbs as lithe
As is the velvet muscle of the pard,
Mephibosheth had been too fair for man.

As if he were a vision that would fade,
Rizpah gazed on him. Never, to her eye,
Grew his bright form familiar; but, like stars,
That seem'd each night new lit in a new heaven,
He was each morn's sweet gift to her. She loved

Her firstborn, as a mother loves her child,
Tenderly, fondly. But for him—the last—
What had she done for heaven to be his mother!
Her heart rose in her throat to hear his voice;
She look'd at him forever through her tears;
Her utterance, when she spoke to him, sank down,
As if the lightest thought of him had lain
In an unfathom'd cavern of her soul.
The morning light was part of him, to her—
What broke the day for, but to show his beauty?
The hours but measured time till he should come;
Too tardy sang the bird when he was gone;
She would have shut the flowers—and call'd the star
Back to the mountain-top—and bade the sun
Pause at eve's golden door—to wait for him!
Was this a heart gone wild?—or is the love
Of mothers like a madness? Such as this
Is many a poor one in her humble home,
Who silently and sweetly sits alone,
Pouring her life all out upon her child.
What cares she that he does not feel how close
Her heart beats after his—that all unseen
Are the fond thoughts that follow him by day,
And watch his sleep like angels? And, when moved
By some sore needed Providence, he stops
In his wild path and lifts a thought to heaven,

What cares the mother that he does not see!
The link between the blessing and her prayer

He who once wept with Mary—angels keeping
Their unthank'd watch—are a foreshadowing
Of what love is in heaven. We may believe
That we shall know each other's forms hereafter,
And, in the bright fields of the better land,
Call the lost dead to us. Oh conscious heart!
That in the lone paths of this shadowy world
Hast bless'd all light, however dimly shining,
That broke upon the darkness of thy way—
Number thy lamps of love, and tell me, now,
How many canst thou re-light at the stars
And blush not at their burning? One—one only—
Lit while your pulses by one heart kept time,
And fed with faithful fondness to your grave—
(Tho' sometimes with a hand stretch'd back from
heaven,)
Steadfast thro' all things—near, when most for-
got—
And with its fingers of unerring truth
Pointing the lost way in thy darkest hour—
One lamp—*thy mother's love*—amid the stars
Shall lift its pure flame changeless, and, before
The throne of God, burn through eternity—
Holy—as it was lit and lent thee here.

The hand in salutation gently raised
To the bow'd forehead of the princely boy,
Linger'd amid his locks. "I sold," he said,
"My Lybian barb for but a cake of meal—
Lo! this—my mother! As I pass'd the street,
I hid it in my mantle, for there stand
Famishing mothers, with their starving babes,
At every threshold; and wild, desperate men
Prowl, with the eyes of tigers, up and down,
Watching to rob those who, from house to house,
Beg for the dying. Fear not thou, my mother!
Thy sons will be Elijah's ravens to thee!"

[UNFINISHED.]

Lazarus and Mary.

Jesus was there but yesterday. The prints
Of his departing feet were at the door;
His "Peace be with you!" was yet audible
In the rapt porch of Mary's charmed ear;
And, in the low rooms, 'twas as if the air,
Hush'd with his going forth, had been the breath
Of angels left on watch—so conscious still
The place seem'd of his presence! Yet, within,
The family by Jesus loved were weeping,
For Lazarus lay dead.

And Mary sat
By the pale sleeper. He was young to die.
The countenance whereon the Saviour dwelt
With his benignant smile—the soft fair lines
Breathing of hope—were still all eloquent,
Like life well mock'd in marble. That the voice,
Gone from those pallid lips, was heard in heaven,
Toned with unearthly sweetness—that the light,
Quench'd in the closing of those stirless lids,

Was veiling before God its timid fire,
New-lit, and brightening like a star at eve—
That Lazarus, her brother, was in bliss,
Not with this cold clay sleeping—Mary knew.
Her heaviness of heart was not for him!
But close had been the tie by Death divided.
The intertwining locks of that bright hair
That wiped the feet of Jesus—the fair hands
Clasp'd in her breathless wonder while He taught—
Scarce to one pulse thrill'd more in unison,
Than with one soul this sister and her brother
Had lock'd their lives together. In this love,
Hallow'd from stain, the woman's heart of Mary
Was, with its rich affections, all bound up.
Of an unblemish'd beauty, as became
An office by archangels fill'd till now,
She walk'd with a celestial halo clad;
And while, to the Apostles' eyes, it seem'd
She but fulfill'd her errand out of heaven—
Sharing her low roof with the Son of God—
She was a woman, fond and mortal still;
And the deep fervor, lost to passion's fire,
Breathed through the sister's tenderness. In vain
Knew Mary, gazing on that face of clay,
That it was not her brother. He was there—
Swathed in that linen vesture for the grave—
The same loved one in all his comeliness—

And with him to the grave her heart must go.
What though he talk'd of her to angels? nay—
Hover'd in spirit near her?—'twas that arm,
Palsied in death, whose fond caress she knew!
It was that lip of marble with whose kiss,
Morning and eve, love hemm'd the sweet day in
This was the form by the Judean maids
Praised for its palm-like stature, as he walk'd
With her by Kedron in the eventide—
The dead was Lazarus! * * * * *
The burial was over, and the night
Fell upon Bethany—and morn—and noon.
And comforters and mourners went their way—
But death stay'd on! They had been oft alone,
When Lazarus had follow'd Christ to hear
His teachings in Jerusalem; but this
Was more than solitude. The silence now
Was void of expectation. Something felt
Always before, and loved without a name,—
Joy from the air, hope from the opening door,
Welcome and life from off the very walls,—
Seem'd gone—and in the chamber where he lay
There was a fearful and unbreathing hush,
Stiller than night's last hour. So fell on Mary
The shadows all have known, who, from their hearts,
Have released friends to heaven. The parting soul

Spreads wing betwixt the mourner and the sky!
As if its path lay, from the tie last broken,
Straight through the cheering gateway of the sun;
And, to the eye strain'd after, 'tis a cloud
That bars the light from all things.

Now as Christ
Drew near to Bethany, the Jews went forth
With Martha, mourning Lazarus. But Mary
Sat in the house. She knew the hour was nigh
When He would go again, as He had said,
Unto his Father; and she felt that He,
Who loved her brother Lazarus in life,
Had chose the hour to bring him home thro' Death
In no unkind forgetfulness. Alone—
She could lift up the bitter prayer to heaven,
"Thy will be done, O God!"—but that dear brother
Had fill'd the cup and broke the bread for Christ;
And ever, at the morn, when she had knelt
And wash'd those holy feet, came Lazarus
To bind his sandals on, and follow forth
With dropp'd eyes, like an angel, sad and fair—
Intent upon the Master's need alone.
Indissolubly link'd were they! And now,
To go to meet him—Lazarus not there—
And to his greeting answer "It is well!"
And, without tears, (since grief would trouble Him

Whose soul was always sorrowful,) to kneel
And minister alone—her heart gave way!
She cover'd up her face and turn'd again
To wait within for Jesus. But once more
Came Martha, saying, "Lo! the Lord is here
And calleth for thee, Mary!" Then arose
The mourner from the ground, whereon she sate
Shrouded in sackcloth, and bound quickly up
The golden locks of her dishevell'd hair,
And o'er her ashy garments drew a veil
Hiding the eyes she could not trust. And still,
As she made ready to go forth, a calm
As in a dream fell on her.

At a fount
Hard by the sepulchre, without the wall,
Jesus awaited Mary. Seated near
Were the way-worn disciples in the shade;
But, of himself forgetful, Jesus lean'd
Upon his staff, and watch'd where she should come
To whose one sorrow—but a sparrow's falling—
The pity that redeem'd a world could bleed!
And as she came, with that uncertain step,—
Eager, yet weak,—her hands upon her breast,—
And they who follow'd her all fallen back
To leave her with her sacred grief alone,—
The heart of Christ was troubled. She drew near,

And the disciples rose up from the fount,
Moved by her look of wo, and gather'd round;
And Mary—for a moment—ere she look'd
Upon the Saviour, stay'd her faltering feet,—
And straighten'd her veil'd form, and tighter drew
Her clasp upon the folds across her breast;
Then, with a vain strife to control her tears,
She stagger'd to their midst, and at His feet
Fell prostrate, saying, "Lord! hadst thou been here,
My brother had not died!" The Saviour groan'd
In spirit, and stoop'd tenderly, and raised
The mourner from the ground, and in a voice,
Broke in its utterance like her own, He said,
"Where have ye laid him?" Then the Jews who came,
Following Mary, answer'd through their tears,
"Lord! come and see!" But lo! the mighty heart
That in Gethsemane sweat drops of blood,
Taking for us the cup that might not pass—
The heart whose breaking cord upon the cross
Made the earth tremble, and the sun afraid
To look upon his agony—the heart
Of a lost world's Redeemer—overflow'd,
Touch'd by a mourner's sorrow! Jesus wept.

Calm'd by those pitying tears, and fondly brooding

Upon the thought that Christ so loved her brother,
Stood Mary there ; but that lost burden now
Lay on His heart who pitied her ; and Christ,
Following slow, and groaning in Himself,
Came to the sepulchre. It was a cave,
And a stone lay upon it. Jesus said,
"Take ye away the stone!" Then lifted He
His moisten'd eyes to heaven, and while the Jews
And the disciples bent their heads in awe,
And trembling Mary sank upon her knees,
The Son of God pray'd audibly. He ceased,
And for a minute's space there was a hush,
As if th' angelic watchers of the world
Had stay'd the pulses of all breathing things,
To listen to that prayer. The face of Christ
Shone as He stood, and over Him there came
Command, as 'twere the living face of God,
And with a loud voice, He cried, "Lazarus!
Come forth!" And instantly, bound hand and foot,
And borne by unseen angels from the cave,
He that was dead stood with them. At the word
Of Jesus, the fear-stricken Jews unloosed
The bands from off the foldings of his shroud;
And Mary, with her dark veil thrown aside,
Ran to him swiftly, and cried, "LAZARUS!
MY BROTHER, LAZARUS!" and tore away
The napkin she had bound about his head—

And touch'd the warm lips with her fearful hand—
And on his neck fell weeping. And while all
Lay on their faces prostrate, Lazarus
Took Mary by the hand, and they knelt down
And worshipp'd Him who loved them.

Thoughts while making the Grave of a New-born Child.

Room, gentle flowers! my child would pass to heaven!
Ye look'd not for her yet with your soft eyes,
O watchful ushers at Death's narrow door!
But lo! while you delay to let her forth,
Angels, beyond, stay for her! One long kiss
From lips all pale with agony, and tears,
Wrung after anguish had dried up with fire
The eyes that wept them, were the cup of life
Held as a welcome to her. Weep! oh mother!
But not that from this cup of bitterness
A cherub of the sky has turn'd away.

One look upon thy face ere thou depart!
My daughter! It is soon to let thee go!
My daughter! With thy birth has gush'd a spring
I knew not of—filling my heart with tears,
And turning with strange tenderness to thee—
A love—oh God! it seems so—that must flow

Far as thou fleest, and 'twixt heaven and me,
Henceforward, be a bright and yearning chain
Drawing me after thee! And so, farewell!
'Tis a harsh world, in which affection knows
No place to treasure up its loved and lost
But the foul grave! Thou, who so late wast sleeping
Warm in the close fold of a mother's heart,
Scarce from her breast a single pulse receiving
But it was sent thee with some tender thought,
How can I leave thee—*here!* Alas for man!
The herb in its humility may fall
And waste into the bright and genial air,
While we—by hands that minister'd in life
Nothing but love to us—are thrust away—
The earth flung in upon our just cold bosoms,
And the warm sunshine trodden out forever!

Yet have I chosen for thy grave, my child,
A bank where I have lain in summer hours,
And thought how little it would seem like death
To sleep amid such loveliness. The brook,
Tripping with laughter down the rocky steps
That lead up to thy bed, would still trip on,
Breaking the dread hush of the mourners gone;
The birds are never silent that build here,
Trying to sing down the more vocal waters:

The slope is beautiful with moss and flowers,
And far below, seen under arching leaves,
Glitters the warm sun on the village spire,
Pointing the living after thee. And this
Seems like a comfort; and, replacing now
The flowers that have made room for thee, I go
To whisper the same peace to ner who lies—
Robb'd of her child and lonely. 'Tis the work
Of many a dark hour, and of many a prayer,
To bring the heart back from an infant gone.
Hope must give o'er, and busy fancy blot
The images from all the silent rooms,
And every sight and sound familiar to her
Undo its sweetest link—and so at last
The fountain—that, once struck, must flow forever—
Will hide and waste in silence. When the smile
Steals to her pallid lip again, and spring
Wakens the buds above thee, we will come,
And, standing by thy music-haunted grave,
Look on each other cheerfully, and say:—
A child that we have loved is gone to heaven,
And by this gate of flowers she pass'd away!

On the Departure of Rev. Mr. White

FROM HIS PARISH, WHEN CHOSEN PRESIDENT OF WABASH COLLEGE.

LEAVE us not, man of prayer! Like Paul, hast thou
"Served God with all humility of mind."
Dwelling among us, and "with many tears,"
"From house to house," "by night and day not ceasing,"
Hast pleaded thy blest errand. Leave us not!
Leave us not now! The Sabbath-bell, so long
Link'd with thy voice—the prelude to thy prayer—
The call to us from heaven to come with thee
Into the house of God, and, from thy lips,
Hear what had fall'n upon thy heart—will sound
Lonely and mournfully when thou art gone!
Our prayers are in thy words—our hope in Christ
Warm'd on thy lips—our darkling thoughts of God
Follow'd thy loved call upward—and so knit
Is all our worship with those outspread hands,
And the imploring voice, which, well we knew,

Sank in the ear of Jesus—that, with thee,
The angel's ladder seems removed from sight,
And we astray in darkness! Leave us not!
Leave not the dead! They have lain calmly down—
Thy comfort in their ears—believing well
That when thine own more holy work was done,
Thou wouldst lie down beside them, and be near
When the last trump shall summon, to fold up
Thy flock affrighted, and, with that same voice
Whose whisper'd promises could sweeten death,
Take up once more the interrupted strain,
And wait Christ's coming, saying, "Here am I,
And those whom thou hast given me!" Leave not
The old, who, 'mid the gathering shadows, cling
To their accustom'd staff, and know not how
To lose thee, and so near the darkest hour!
Leave not the penitent, whose soul may be
Deaf to the strange voice, but awake to thine!
Leave not the mourner thou hast sooth'd—the heart
Turns to its comforter again! Leave not
The child thou hast baptized! another's care
May not keep bright, upon the mother's heart,
The covenant seal; the infant's ear has caught
Words it has strangely ponder'd from thy lips,
And the remember'd tone may find again,

And quicken for the harvest, the first seed
Sown for eternity! Leave not the child!

Yet if thou wilt—if, "bound in spirit," thou
Must go, and we shall see thy face no more,
"The will of God be done!" We do not say
Remember us—thou wilt—in love and prayer!
And thou wilt be remember'd—by *the dead*,
When the last trump awakes them—by *the old*,
When, of the "silver cord" whose strength thou
knowest,
The last thread fails—by *the bereaved and stricken*,
When the dark cloud, wherein thou found'st a spot
Broke by the light of mercy, lowers again—
By *the sad mother*, pleading for her child,
In murmurs difficult, since thou art gone—
By *all thou leavest*, when the Sabbath-bell
Brings us together, and the closing hymn
Hushes our hearts to pray, and thy loved voice,
That all our wants had grown to, (only thus,
'Twould seem, articulate to God,) falls not
Upon our listening ears—remember'd thus—
Remember'd well—in all our holiest hours—
Will be the faithful shepherd we have lost!
And ever with one prayer, for which our love
Will find the pleading words,—that in the light
Of heaven we may behold his face once more!

Birth-day Verses.

"The heart that we have lain near before our birth, is the only one that cannot forget that it has loved us."

Philip Slingsby.

My birth-day !—Oh beloved mother !
  My heart is with thee o'er the seas.
I did not think to count another
  Before I wept upon thy knees—
Before this scroll of absent years
Was blotted with thy streaming tears

My own I do not care to check.
  I weep—albeit here alone—
As if I hung upon thy neck,
  As if thy lips were on my own,
As if this full, sad heart of mine,
Were beating closely upon thine.

Four weary years ! How looks she now ?
  What light is in those tender eyes ?

What trace of time has touch'd the brow
Whose look is borrow'd of the skies
That listen to her nightly prayer?
How is she changed since *he* was there
Who sleeps upon her heart alway—
Whose name upon her lips is worn—
For whom the night seems made to pray—
For whom she wakes to pray at morn—
Whose sight is dim, whose heart-strings stir,
Who weeps these tears—to think of *her!*

I know not if my mother's eyes
Would find me changed in slighter things;
I've wander'd beneath many skies,
And tasted of some bitter springs;
And many leaves, once fair and gay,
From youth's full flower have dropp'd away—
But, as these looser leaves depart,
The lessen'd flower gets near the core,
And, when deserted quite, the heart
Takes closer what was dear of yore—
And yearns to those who loved it first—
The sunshine and the dew by which its bud was nursed.

Dear mother! dost thou love me yet?
Am I remember'd in my home?

When those I love for joy are met,
  Does some one wish that I would come?
Thou *dost*—I *am* beloved of these!
  But, as the schoolboy numbers o'er
Night after night the Pleiades
  And finds the stars he found before—
As turns the maiden oft her token—
  As counts the miser aye his gold—
So, till life's silver cord is broken,
  Would I of thy fond love be told.
My heart is full, mine eyes are wet—
Dear mother! dost thou love thy long-lost wanderer yet?

Oh! when the hour to meet again
  Creeps on—and, speeding o'er the sea,
My heart takes up its lengthen'd chain,
  And, link by link, draws nearer thee—
When land is hail'd, and, from the shore,
  Comes off the blessed breath of home,
With fragrance from my mother's door
  Of flowers forgotten when I come—
When port is gain'd, and slowly now,
  The old familiar paths are pass'd,
And, entering—unconscious how—
  I gaze upon thy face at last,
And run to thee, all faint and weak,

And feel thy tears upon my cheek—
  Oh! if my heart break not with joy,
The light of heaven will fairer seem;
  And I shall grow once more a boy:
And, mother!—'twill be like a dream
  That we were parted thus for years,—
  And once that we have dried our tears,
  How will the days seem long and bright—
To meet thee always with the morn,
  And hear thy blessing every night—
Thy "dearest," thy "first-born!"—
And be no more, as now, in a strange land, forlorn!

To my Mother from the Appenines.

Mother! dear mother! the feelings nurst
As I hung at thy bosom, *clung round thee first.*
'Twas the earliest link in love's warm chain—
'Tis the only one that will long remain:
And as year by year, and day by day,
Some friend still trusted drops away,
Mother! dear mother! *oh dost thou see*
How the shorten'd chain brings me nearer thee!

Early Poems

'Tis midnight the lone mountains on—
The East is fleck'd with cloudy bars,
And, gliding through them one by one,
The moon walks up her path of stars—
The light upon her placid brow
Received from fountains unseen now.

And happiness is mine to-night,
Thus springing from an unseen fount;
And breast and brain are warm with light,
With midnight round me on the mount—

Its rays, like thine, fair Dian, flow
From that far Western star below.

Dear mother! in thy love I live;
  The life thou gav'st flows yet from thee—
And, sun-like, thou hast power to give
  Life to the earth, air, sea, for me!
Though wandering, as this moon above,
I'm dark without thy constant love.

Lines on leaving Europe.

Bright flag at yonder tapering mast!
  Fling out your field of azure blue;
Let star and stripe be westward cast,
  And point as Freedom's eagle flew!
Strain home! oh lithe and quivering spars!
Point home, my country's flag of stars!

The wind blows fair! the vessel feels
  The pressure of the rising breeze,
And, swiftest of a thousand keels,
  She leaps to the careering seas!
Oh, fair, fair cloud of snowy sail,
  In whose white breast I seem to lie,
How oft, when blew this eastern gale,
  I've seen your semblance in the sky,
And long'd with breaking heart to flee
On cloud-like pinions o'er the sea!

Adieu, oh lands of fame and eld!
  I turn to watch our foamy track,

And thoughts with which I first beheld
  Yon clouded line, come hurrying back;
My lips are dry with vague desire,—
  My cheek once more is hot with joy—
My pulse, my brain, my soul on fire!—
  Oh, what has changed that traveller-boy!
As leaves the ship this dying foam,
His visions fade behind—his weary heart speeds home!

Adieu, oh soft and southern shore,
  Where dwelt the stars long miss'd in heaven—
Those forms of beauty seen no more,
  Yet once to Art's rapt vision given!
Oh, still th' enamor'd sun delays,
  And pries through fount and crumbling fane,
To win to his adoring gaze
  Those children of the sky again!
Irradiate beauty, such as never
  That light on other earth hath shone,
Hath made this land her home forever;
  And could I live for this alone—
Were not my birthright brighter far
  Than such voluptuous slaves, can be—
Held not the West one glorious star
  New-born and blazing for the free—
Soar'd not to heaven our eagle yet—

Rome, with her Helot sons, should teach me to forget!

Adieu, oh fatherland! I see
Your white cliffs on th' horizon's rim,
And though to freer skies I flee
My heart swells, and my eyes are dim!
As knows the dove the task you give her,
When loosed upon a foreign shore—
As spreads the rain-drop in the river
In which it may have flow'd before—
To England, over vale and mountain,
My fancy flew from climes more fair—
My blood, that knew its parent fountain,
Ran warm and fast in England's air.

Dear mother! in thy prayer, to-night,
There come new words and warmer tears!
On long, long darkness breaks the light—
Comes home the loved, the lost for years!
Sleep safe, oh wave-worn mariner!
Fear not, to-night, or storm or sea!
The ear of heaven bends low to *her!*
He comes to shore who sails with me!
The spider knows the roof unriven,
While swings his web, though lightnings blaze—

And by a thread still fast on heaven,
  I know my mother lives and prays!

Dear mother! when our lips can speak—
  When first our tears will let us see—
When I can gaze upon thy cheek,
  And thou, with thy dear eyes, on me—
'Twill be a pastime little sad
  To trace what weight Time's heavy fingers
Upon each other's forms have had—
  For all may flee, so feeling lingers!
But there's a change, beloved mother!
  To stir far deeper thoughts of thine;
I come—but with me comes another
  To share the heart once only mine!
Thou, on whose thoughts, when sad and lonely,
  One star arose in memory's heaven—
Thou, who hast watch'd *one* treasure only—
  Water'd *one* flower with tears at even—
Room in thy heart! The hearth she left
  Is darken'd to lend light to ours!
There are bright flowers of care bereft,
  And hearts—that languish more than flowers!
She was their light—their very air—
Room, mother! in thy heart! place for her in thy prayer!

A true Incident.

Upon a summer's morn, a southern mother
Sat at the curtain'd window of an inn.
She rested from long travel, and with hand
Upon her cheek in tranquil happiness,
Look'd where the busy travellers went and came.
And, like the shadows of the swallows flying
Over the bosom of unruffled water,
Pass'd from her thoughts all objects, leaving there,
As in the water's breast, a mirror'd heaven—
For, in the porch beneath her, to and fro,
A nurse walk'd singing with her babe in arms.
And many a passer-by look'd on the child
And praised its wondrous beauty, but still on
The old nurse troll'd her lullaby, and still,
Blest through her depths of soul by light there shining,
The mother in her revery mused on.
But lo! another traveller alighted!
And now, no more indifferent or calm,

The mother's breath comes quick, and with the blood
Warm in her cheek and brow, she murmurs low,
" Now, God be praised! I am no more alone
In knowing I've an angel for my child,—
Chance he to look on't only!" With a smile—
The tribute of a beauty-loving heart
To things from God new-moulded—would have pass'd
The poet, as the infant caught his eye;
But suddenly he turn'd, and with his hand
Upon the nurse's arm, he stay'd her steps,
And gazed upon her burthen. 'Twas a child
In whose large eyes of blue there shone, indeed,
Something to waken wonder. Never sky
In noontide depth, or softly-breaking dawn—
Never the dew in new-born violet's cup,
Lay so entranced in purity! Not calm,
With the mere hush of infancy at rest,
The ample forehead, but serene with thought;
And by the rapt expression of the lips,
They seem'd scarce still from a cherubic hymn;
And over all its countenance there breathed
Benignity, majestic as we dream
Angels wear ever, before God. With gaze
Earnest and mournful, and his eyelids warm
With tears kept back, the poet kiss'd the child;

And chasten'd at his heart, as having pass'd
Close to an angel, went upon his way.
  Soon after, to the broken choir in heaven
This cherub was recall'd, and now the mother
Bethought her, in her anguish, of the bard—
(Herself a far-off stranger, but his heart
Familiar to the world,)—and wrote to tell him,
The angel he had recognised that morn,
Had fled to bliss again. The poet well
Remember'd that child's ministry to him;
And of the only fountain that he knew
For healing, he sought comfort for the mother.
And thus he wrote:—

Mourn not for the child from thy tenderness riven,
  Ere stain on its purity fell!
To thy questioning heart, lo! an answer from heaven:
  "IS IT WELL WITH THE CHILD?" "IT IS WELL!"

The Mother to her Child.

THEY tell me thou art come from a far world,
Babe of my bosom! that these little arms,
Whose restlessness is like the spread of wings,
Move with the memory of flighst scarce o'er—
That through these fringed lids we see the soul
Steep'd in the blue of its remember'd home;
And while thou sleep'st come messengers, they
say,
Whispering to thee—and 'tis then I see
Upon thy baby lips that smile of heaven!
And what is thy far errand, my fair child?
Why away, wandering from a home of bliss,
To find thy way through darkness home again?
Wert thou an untried dweller in the sky?
Is there, betwixt the cherub that thou wert,
The cherub and the angel thou mayst be,
A life's probation in this sadder world?
Art thou with memory of two things only,
Music and light, left upon earth astray,
And, by the watchers at the gate of heaven,

Look'd for with fear and trembling?
God! who gavest
Into my guiding hand this wanderer,
To lead her through a world whose darkling paths
I tread with steps so faltering—leave not me
To bring her to the gates of heaven alone!
I feel my feebleness. Let *these* stay on—
The angels who now visit her in dreams!
Bid them be near her pillow till in death
The closed eyes look upon Thy face once more!
And let the light and music, which the world
Borrows of heaven, and which her infant sense
Hails with sweet recognition, be to her
A voice to call her upward, and a lamp
To lead her steps unto Thee!

A Thought over a Cradle.

I SADDEN when thou smilest to my smile,
Child of my love! I tremble to believe
That o'er the mirror of that eye of blue
The shadow of my heart will always pass,—
A heart that, from its struggle with the world,
Comes nightly to thy guarded cradle home,
And, careless of the staining dust it brings,
Asks for its idol! Strange that flowers of earth
Are visited by every air that stirs,
And drink in sweetness only, while the child
That shuts within its breast a bloom for heaven,
May take a blemish from the breath of love,
And bear the blight forever.
I have wept
With gladness at the gift of this fair child!
My life is bound up in her. But, oh God!
Thou know'st how heavily my heart at times
Bears its sweet burthen; and if thou hast given
To nurture such as mine this spotless flower,
To bring it unpolluted unto thee,

Take thou its love, I pray thee! Give it light—
Though, following the sun, it turn from me!—
But, by the chord thus wrung, and by the light
Shining about her, draw me to my child!
And link us close, oh God, when near to heaven!

Thirty-five.

"The years of a man's life are threescore and ten."

Oh, weary heart! thou'rt half-way home!
  We stand on life's meridian height—
As far from childhood's morning come,
  As to the grave's forgetful night.
Give Youth and Hope a parting tear—
  Look onward with a placid brow—
Hope promised but to bring us here,
  And Reason takes the guidance now—
One backward look—the last—the last!
One silent tear—for *Youth is past!*

Who goes with Hope and Passion back?
  Who comes with me and Memory on?
Oh, lonely looks the downward track—
  Joy's music hush'd—Hope's roses gone!
To Pleasure and her giddy troop
  Farewell, without a sigh or tear!
But heart gives way, and spirits droop,
  To think that Love may leave us here!

Have we no charm when Youth is flown—
Midway to death left sad and lone!

Yet stay!—as 'twere a twilight star
That sends its thread across the wave,
I see a brightening light, from far,
Steal down a path beyond the grave!
And now—bless God!—its golden line
Comes o'er—and lights my shadowy way—
And shows the dear hand clasp'd in mine!
But, list what those sweet voices say!
The better land's in sight,
And, by its chastening light,
All love from life's midway is driven,
Save hers whose claspèd hand will bring thee on to heaven!

Contemplation.

"They are all up—the innumerable stars—
And hold their place in heaven. My eyes have
been
Searching the pearly depths through which they
spring
Like beautiful creations, till I feel
As if it were a new and perfect world,
Waiting in silence for the word of God
To breathe it into motion. There they stand,
Shining in order, like a living hymn
Written in light, awaking at the breath
Of the celestial dawn, and praising Him
Who made them, with the harmony of spheres.
I would I had an eagle's ear to list
That melody. I would that I might float
Up in that boundless element and feel
Its ravishing vibrations, like the pulse
Beating in heaven! My spirit is athirst
For music—rarer music! I would bathe

My soul in a serener atmosphere
Than this ; I long to mingle with the flock
Led by the 'living waters,' and to stray
In the 'green pastures' of the better land!
When wilt thou break, dull fetter! When shall I
Gather my wings, and like a rushing thought
Stretch onward, star by star, up into heaven!"
Thus mused Alethe. She was one to whom
Life had been like the witching of a dream,
Of an untroubled sweetness. She was born
Of a high race, and lay upon the knee.
With her soft eyes perusing listlessly
The fretted roof, or, on Mosaic floors,
Grasp'd at the tesselated squares inwrought
With metals curiously. Her childhood pass'd
Like faery—amid fountains and green haunts—
Trying her little feet upon a lawn
Of velvet evenness, and hiding flowers
In her sweet breast, as if it were a fair
And pearly altar to crush incense on.
Her youth—oh! that was queenly! She was like
A dream of poetry that may not be
Written or told—exceeding beautiful!
And so came worshippers ; and rank bow'd down
And breathed upon her heart-strings with the breath
Of pride, and bound her forehead gorgeously

With dazzling scorn, and gave unto her step
A majesty—as if she trod the sea,
And the proud waves, unbidden, lifted her!
And so she grew to woman—her mere look
Strong as a monarch's signet, and her hand
The ambition of a kingdom. From all this
Turn'd her high heart away! She had a mind,
Deep, and immortal, and it would not feed
On pageantry. She thirsted for a spring
Of a serener element, and drank
Philosophy, and for a little while
She was allay'd,—till, presently, it turn'd
Bitter within her, and her spirit grew
Faint for undying water. Then she came
To the pure fount of God, and is athirst
No more—save when the fever of the world
Falleth upon her, she will go, sometimes,
Out in the star-light quietness, and breathe
A holy aspiration after Heaven.

On the Death of a Missionary.

How beautiful it is for man to die
Upon the walls of Zion! to be call'd,
Like a watch-worn and weary sentinel,
To put his armor off, and rest—in heaven!

The sun was setting on Jerusalem,
The deep blue sky had not a cloud, and light
Was pouring on the dome of Omar's mosque,
Like molten silver. Every thing was fair;
And beauty hung upon the painted fanes;
Like a grieved spirit, lingering ere she gave
Her wing to air, for heaven. The crowds of men
Were in the busy streets, and nothing look'd
Like wo, or suffering, save one small train
Bearing the dead to burial. It pass'd by,
And left no trace upon the busy throng.
The sun was just as beautiful; the shout
Of joyous revelry, and the low hum
Of stirring thousands rose as constantly!
Life look'd as winning; and the earth and sky,

And every thing seem'd strangely bent to make
A contrast to that comment upon life.
How wonderful it is that human pride
Can pass that touching moral as it does—
Pass it so frequently, in all the force
Of mournful and most simple eloquence—
And learn no lesson! They bore on the dead,
With the slow step of sorrow, troubled not
By the rude multitude, save, here and there,
A look of vague inquiry, or a curse
Half-mutter'd by some haughty Turk whose sleeve
Had touch'd the tassel of the Christian's pall.
And Israel too pass'd on—the trampled Jew!
Israel!—who made Jerusalem a throne
For the wide world—pass'd on as carelessly;
Giving no look of interest to tell
The shrouded dead was any thing to her.
Oh that they would be gather'd as a brood
Is gather'd by a parent's sheltering wings!—

They laid him down with strangers; for his home
Was with the setting sun, and they who stood
And look'd so steadfastly upon his grave,
Were not his kindred; but they found him there,
And loved him for his ministry of Christ.
He had died young. But there are silver'd heads
Whose race of duty is less nobly run.

His heart was with Jerusalem ; and strong
As was a mother's love, and the sweet ties
Religion makes so beautiful at home,
He flung them from him in his eager race,
And sought the broken people of his God,
To preach to them of JESUS. There was one,
Who was his friend and helper. One who went
And knelt beside him at the sepulchre
Where Jesus slept, to pray for Israel.
They had one spirit, and their hearts were knit
With more than human love. God call'd him home.
And he of whom I speak stood up alone,
And in his broken-heartedness wrought on
Until his Master call'd him.

Oh, is it not a noble thing to die
As dies the Christian, with his armor on !—
What is the hero's clarion, though its blast
Ring with the mastery of a world, to this ?—
What are the searching victories of mind—
The lore of vanish'd ages ?—What are all
The trumpetings of proud humanity,
To the short history of him who made
His sepulchre beside the King of kings ?

On the Picture of a "Child tired of Play."

TIRED of play! Tired of play!
What hast thou done this livelong day!
The birds are silent, and so is the bee;
The sun is creeping up steeple and tree;
The doves have flown to the sheltering eaves,
And the nests are dark with the drooping leaves;
Twilight gathers, and day is done—
How hast thou spent it—restless one!

Playing? But what hast thou done beside
To tell thy mother at eventide?
What promise of morn is left unbroken?
What kind word to thy playmate spoken?
Whom hast thou pitied, and whom forgiven?
How with thy faults has duty striven?
What hast thou learn'd by field and hill,
By greenwood path, and by singing rill

There will come an eve to a longer day,

That will find thee tired—but not of play!
And thou wilt lean, as thou leanest now,
With drooping limbs and aching brow,
And wish the shadows would faster creep,
And long to go to thy quiet sleep.
Well were it then if thine aching brow
Were as free from sin and shame as now!
Well for thee, if thy lip could tell
A tale like this, of a day spent well.
If thine open hand hath relieved distress—
If thy pity hath sprung to wretchedness—
If thou hast forgiven the sore offence,
And humbled thy heart with penitence—
If Nature's voices have spoken to thee
With her holy meanings eloquently—
If every creature hath won thy love,
From the creeping worm to the brooding dove—
If never a sad, low-spoken word
Hath plead with thy human heart unheard—
Then when the night steals on, as now,
It will bring relief to thine aching brow,
And, with joy and peace at the thought of rest,
Thou wilt sink to sleep on thy mother's breast.

A Child's first Impression of a Star.

She had been told that God made all the stars
That twinkled up in heaven, and now she stood
Watching the coming of the twilight on,
As if it were a new and perfect world,
And this were its first eve. She stood alone
By the low window, with the silken lash
Of her soft eye upraised, and her sweet mouth
Half parted with the new and strange delight
Of beauty that she could not comprehend,
And had not seen before. The purple folds
Of the low sunset clouds, and the blue sky
That look'd so still and delicate above,
Fill'd her young heart with gladness, and the eve
Stole on with its deep shadows, and she still
Stood looking at the west with that half smile,
As if a pleasant thought were at her heart.
Presently, in the edge of the last tint
Of sunset, where the blue was melted in
To the faint golden mellowness, a star

Stood suddenly. A laugh of wild delight
Burst from her lips, and putting up her hands,
Her simple thought broke forth expressively—
"Father! dear father! God has made a star!"

On Witnessing a Baptism.

SHE stood up in the meekness of a heart
Resting on God, and held her fair young child
Upon her bosom, with its gentle eyes
Folded in sleep, as if its soul had gone
To whisper the baptismal vow in heaven.
The prayer went up devoutly, and the lips
Of the good man glow'd fervently with faith
That it would be, even as he had pray'd,
And the sweet child be gather'd to the fold
Of Jesus. As the holy words went on
Her lips moved silently, and tears, fast tears,
Stole from beneath her lashes, and upon
The forehead of the beautiful child lay soft
With the baptismal water. Then I thought
That to the eye of God, that mother's tears
Would be a deeper covenant—which sin
And the temptations of the world, and death
Would leave unbroken—and that she would know

In the clear light of heaven, how very strong
The prayer which press'd them from her heart had been
In leading its young spirit up to God.

Reverie at Glenmary.

I HAVE enough, O God! My heart to-night
Runs over with its fulness of content;
And as I look out on the fragrant stars,
And from the beauty of the night take in
My priceless portion—yet myself no more
Than in the universe a grain of sand—
I feel His glory who could make a world,
Yet in the lost depths of the wilderness
Leave not a flower unfinish'd!

Rich, though poor!
My low-roof'd cottage is this hour a heaven.
Music is in it—and the song she sings,
That sweet-voiced wife of mine, arrests the ear
Of my young child awake upon her knee;
And with his calm eye on his master's face,
My noble hound lies couchant—and all here—
All in this little home, yet boundless heaven—
Are, in such love as I have power to give,
Blessed to overflowing.

Thou, who look'st
Upon my brimming heart this tranquil eve,
Knowest its fulness, as thou dost the dew
Sent to the hidden violet by Thee ;
And, as that flower, from its unseen abode,
Sends its sweet breath up, duly, to the sky,
Changing its gift to incense, so, oh God !
May the sweet drops that to my humble cup
Find their far way from heaven, send up, to Thee,
Fragrance at thy throne welcome !

To a City Pigeon.

STOOP to my window, thou beautiful dove!
Thy daily visits have touch'd my love.
I watch thy coming, and list the note
That stirs so low in thy mellow throat,
  And my joy is high
To catch the glance of thy gentle eye.

Why dost thou sit on the heated eaves,
And forsake the wood with its freshen'd leaves?
Why dost thou haunt the sultry street,
When the paths of the forest are cool and sweet?
  How canst thou bear
This noise of people—this sultry air?

Thou alone of the feather'd race
Dost look unscared on the human face;
Thou alone, with a wing to flee,
Dost love with man in his haunts to be;
  And the "gentle dove"
Has become a name for trust and love.

A holy gift is thine, sweet bird!
Thou'rt named with childhood's earliest word!
Thou'rt link'd with all that is fresh and wild
In the prison'd thoughts of the city child;
        And thy glossy wings
Are its brightest image of moving things.

It is no light chance. Thou art set apart,
Wisely by Him who has tamed thy heart,
To stir the love for the bright and fair
That else were seal'd in this crowded air;
        I sometimes dream
Angelic rays from thy pinions stream.

Come then, ever, when daylight leaves
The page I read, to my humble eaves,
And wash thy breast in the hollow spout,
And murmur thy low sweet music out!
        I hear and see
Lessons of heaven, sweet bird, in thee!

The Belfry Pigeon.

On the cross-beam under the Old South bell
The nest of a pigeon is builded well.
In summer and winter that bird is there,
Out and in with the morning air:
I love to see him track the street,
With his wary eye and active feet;
And I often watch him as he springs,
Circling the steeple with easy wings,
Till across the dial his shade has pass'd,
And the belfry edge is gain'd at last.
'Tis a bird I love, with its brooding note,
And the trembling throb in its mottled throat;
There's a human look in its swelling breast,
And the gentle curve of its lowly crest;
And I often stop with the fear I feel—
He runs so close to the rapid wheel.

Whatever is rung on that noisy bell—
Chime of the hour or funeral knell—
The dove in the belfry must hear it well.

When the tongue swings out to the midnight moon—
When the sexton cheerly rings for noon—
When the clock strikes clear at morning light—
When the child is waked with "nine at night"—
When the chimes play soft in the Sabbath air,
Filling the spirit with tones of prayer—
Whatever tale in the bell is heard,
He broods on his folded feet unstirr'd,
Or, rising half in his rounded nest,
He takes the time to smooth his breast,
Then drops again with filmed eyes,
And sleeps as the last vibration dies.
Sweet bird! I would that I could be
A hermit in the crowd like thee!
With wings to fly to wood and glen,
Thy lot, like mine, is cast with men;
And daily, with unwilling feet,
I tread, like thee, the crowded street;
But, unlike me, when day is o'er,
Thou canst dismiss the world and soar,
Or, at a half-felt wish for rest,
Canst smooth the feathers on thy breast,
And drop, forgetful, to thy nest.

Saturday Afternoon.

[*Written for a Picture.*]

I LOVE to look on a scene like this,
  Of wild and careless play,
And persuade myself that I am not old,
  And my locks are not yet gray;
For it stirs the blood in an old man's heart,
  And makes his pulses fly,
To catch the thrill of a happy voice,
  And the light of a pleasant eye.

I have walk'd the world for fourscore years;
  And they say that I am old,
That my heart is ripe for the reaper, Death,
  And my years are well-nigh told.
It is very true; it is very true;
  I'm old, and "I 'bide my time:"
But my heart will leap at a scene like this,
  And I half renew my prime.

Play on, play on; I am with you there,

In the midst of your merry ring;
I can feel the thrill of the daring jump,
And the rush of the breathless swing.
I hide with you in the fragrant hay,
And I whoop the smother'd call,
And my feet slip up on the seedy floor,
And I care not for the fall.

I am willing to die when my time shall come
And I shall be glad to go;
For the world at best is a weary place,
And my pulse is getting low;
But the grave is dark, and the heart will fail
In treading its gloomy way;
And it wiles my heart from its dreariness,
To see the young so gay.

The Sabbath.

It was a pleasant morning, in the time
When the leaves fall—and the bright sun shone
 out
As when the morning stars first sang together—
So quietly and calmly fell his light
Upon a world at rest. There was no leaf
In motion, and the loud winds slept, and all
Was still. The lab'ring herd was grazing
Upon the hill-side quietly—uncall'd
By the harsh voice of man; and distant sound,
Save from the murmuring waterfall, came not
As usual on the ear. One hour stole on,
And then another of the morning, calm
And still as Eden ere the birth of man.
And then broke in the Sabbath chime of bells—
And the old man, and his descendants, went
Together to the house of God. I join'd
The well-apparell'd crowd. The holy man
Rose solemnly, and breathed the prayer of faith—
And the gray saint, just on the wing for heaven—

And the fair maid—and the bright-hair'd young
man—
And child of curling locks, just taught to close
The lash of its blue eye the while ;—all knelt
In attitude of prayer—and then the hymn,
Sincere in its low melody, went up
To worship God.

The white-hair'd pastor rose
And look'd upon his flock—and with an eye
That told his interest, and voice that spoke
In tremulous accents, eloquence like Paul's,
He lent Isaiah's fire to the truths
Of revelation, and persuasion came
Like gushing waters from his lips, till hearts
Unused to bend were soften'd, and the eye
Unwont to weep sent forth the willing tear.

I went my way—but as I went, I thought
How holy was the Sabbath-day of God.

Dedication Hymn.

[*Written to be sung at the consecration of Hanover-street Church, Boston.*]

THE perfect world by Adam trod,
Was the first temple—built by God—
His fiat laid the corner-stone,
And heaved its pillars, one by one.

He hung its starry roof on high—
The broad illimitable sky;
He spread its pavement, green and bright,
And curtain'd it with morning light.

The mountains in their places stood—
The sea—the sky—and "all was good;"
And, when its first pure praises rang,
The "morning stars together sang."

Lord! 'tis not ours to make the sea
And earth and sky a house for thee;
But in thy sight our off'ring stands—
A humbler temple, "made with hands."

www.ingramcontent.com/pod-product-compliance
Lightning Source LLC
LaVergne TN
LVHW021422110826
845150LV00007B/2039

* 9 7 8 1 4 2 5 5 0 8 5 7 9 *